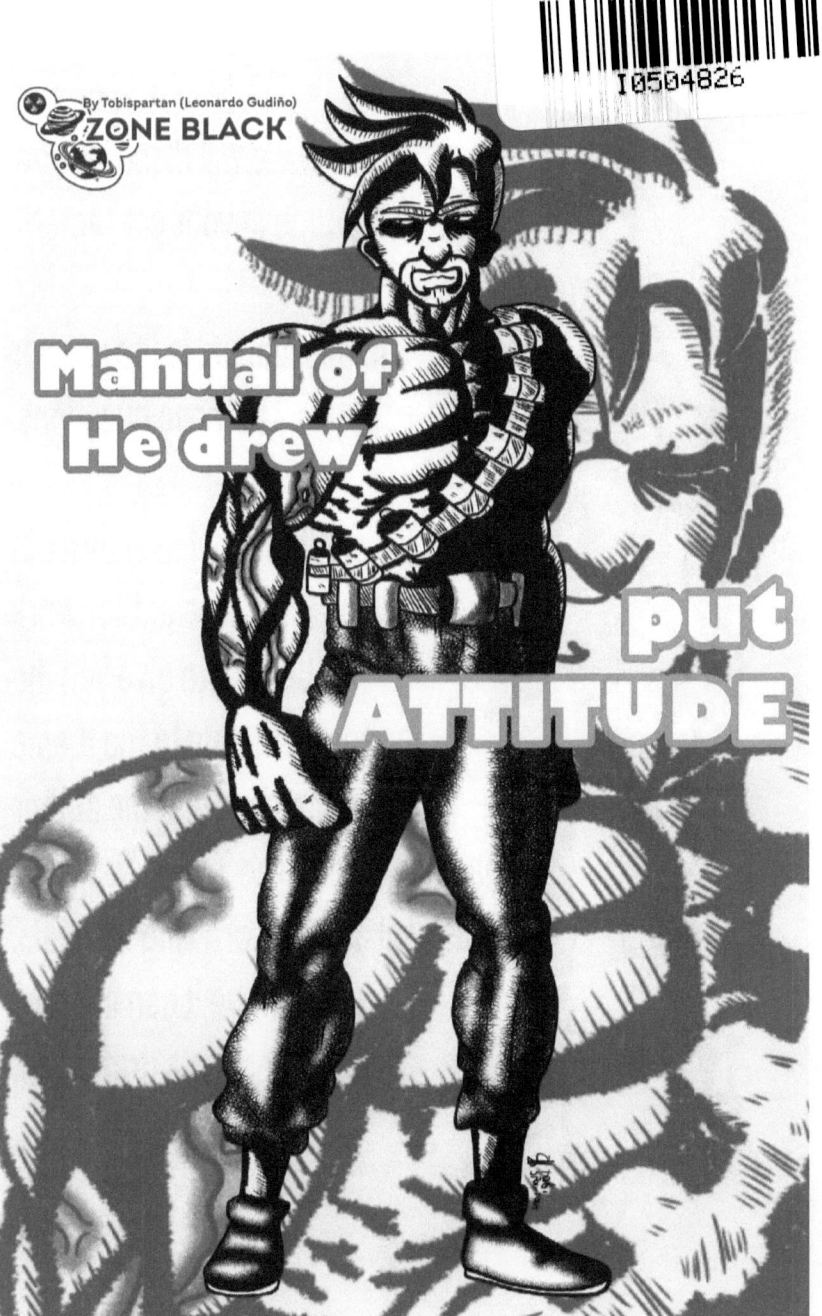

Now we will discover how improve attitude in your characters.

In this manual is the answer to those questions.

Although it may turn out something basic, the author work to be able to give you the better continuity to the theme remember that the author has published "The Tao of Drawing" as well as other drawing manuals, so we hope it can improve your talent as a draftsman.

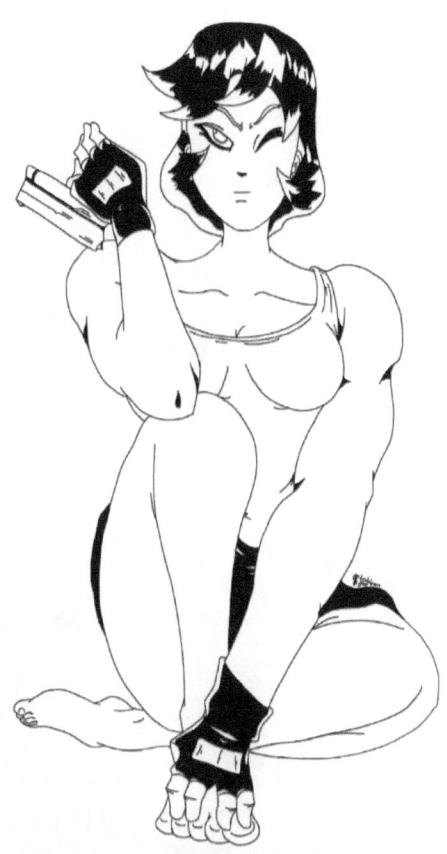

An important point in character design
is to give it a personality consistent with
the main idea you have, here we will see
some postures and gestures
with which you will understand how
give more presence to the actions
of your characters.

3

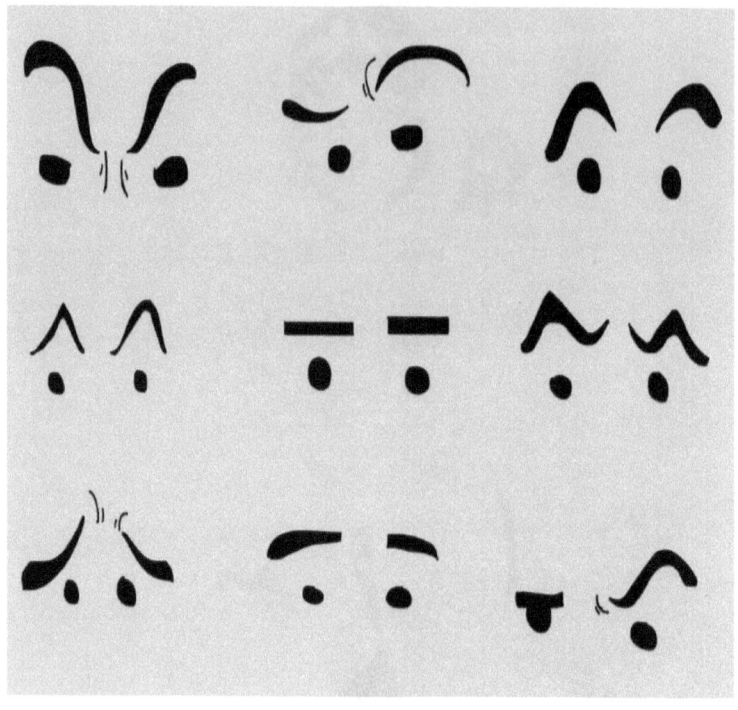

One of the main keys to gesticulation
are the eyebrows, which are very representative
Mood; for example, when
eyebrows meet at the centerline of the face
and they bow down they simulate the shape
from an angry person but when
eyebrows do the opposite effect
they can represent surprise, fright or happiness.

4

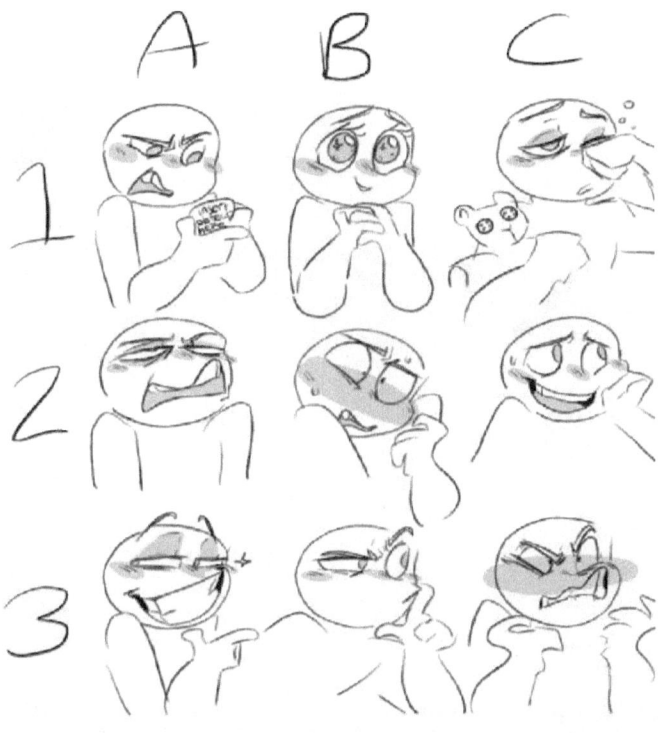

When the eyebrows arch more than normal,
can be represented as an action of
surprise or supplication; when the eyebrows
they stay in a normal posture but
raised a little, could be understood
as a posture of disapproval;
another eyebrow reaction means
strangeness or pride.

5

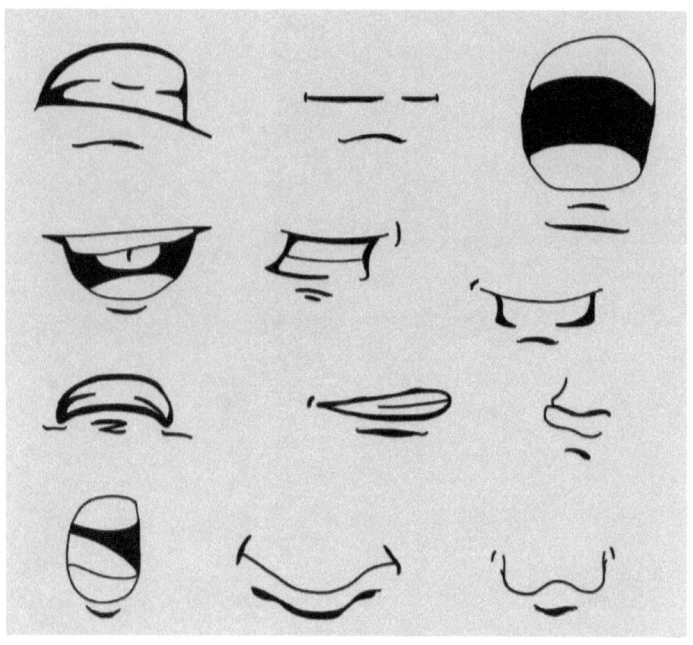

The second most representative point of
emotions is the mouth, and not so much for what
it is said with it, but with the movements
lips and teeth.

The most common mouth movements are
bows, with a bow down
or upwards they can
represent joy or anger.

6

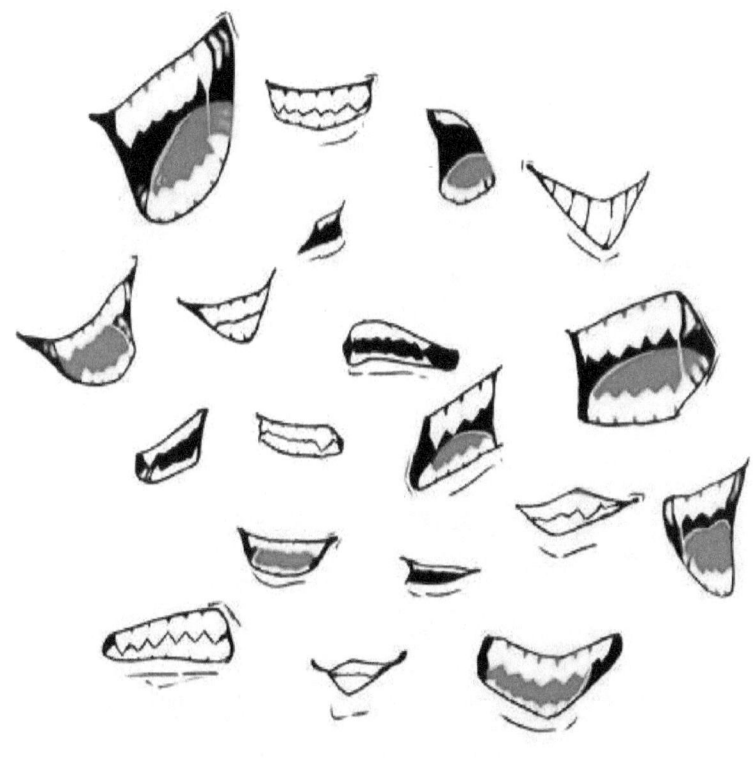

But not everything is bowing, too
you can draw the mouth half open,
oval, elongated, etc.

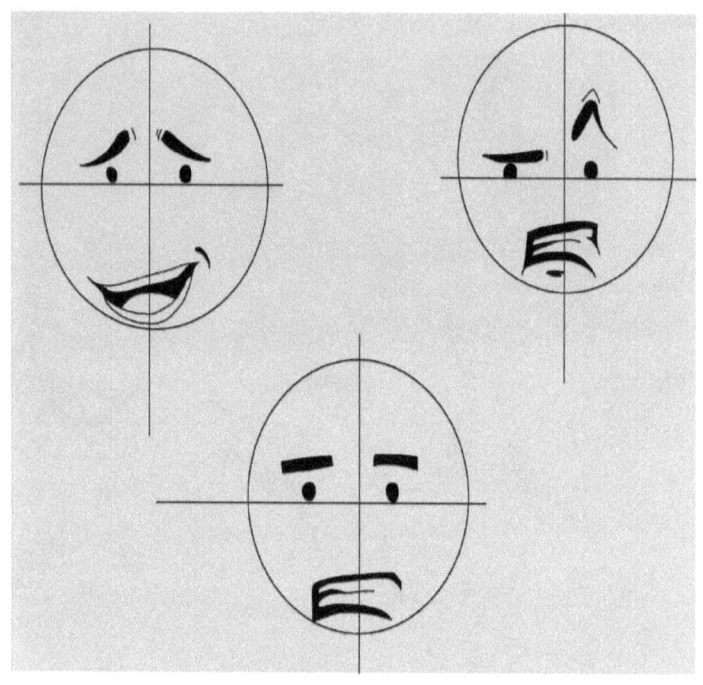

In these examples, you can clearly see the gesticulation of the
mouth and eyebrow movements.

Eyebrows together, eyes narrowed and mouth arched down,
is the expression of anger.

See how expressions such as anguish or joy are resolved.

8

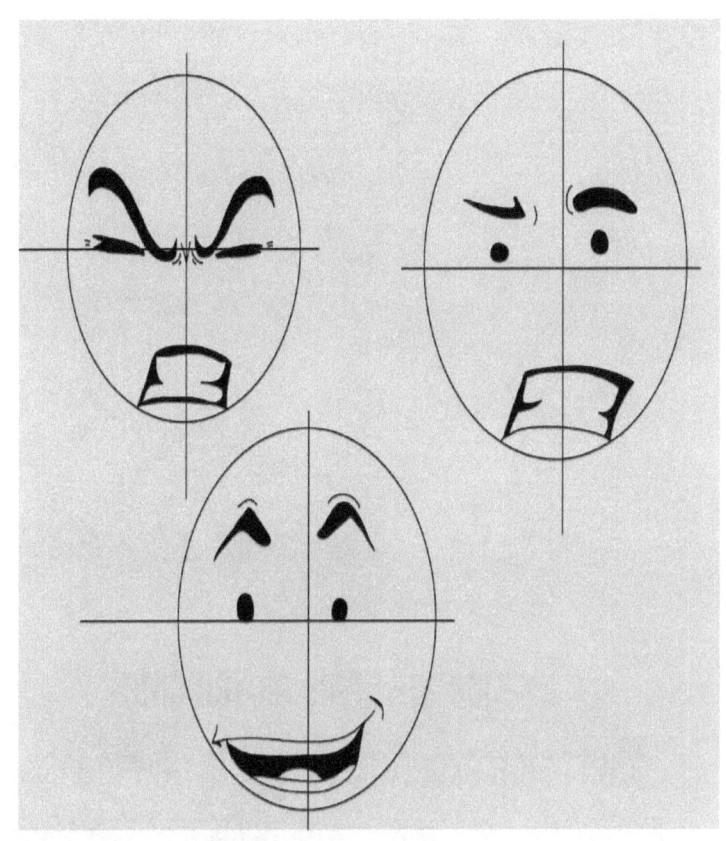

Combine styles of eyebrows and mouths
to get different results every time.

9

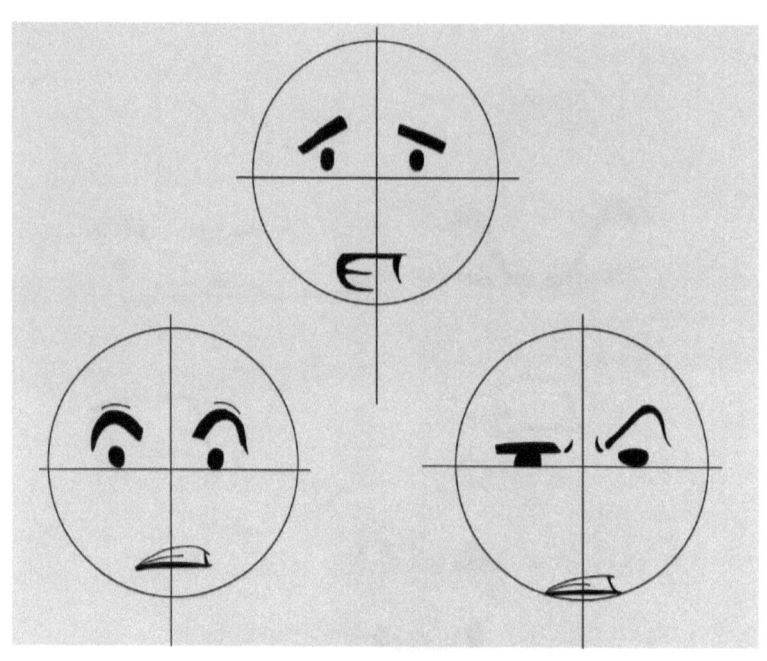

Exaggerate some movements,
don't stop experimenting with new ideas.
Notice that like the mouth the eyebrows have
arc movements, which vary according
to the intention you want to give to the
performance of the character.

10

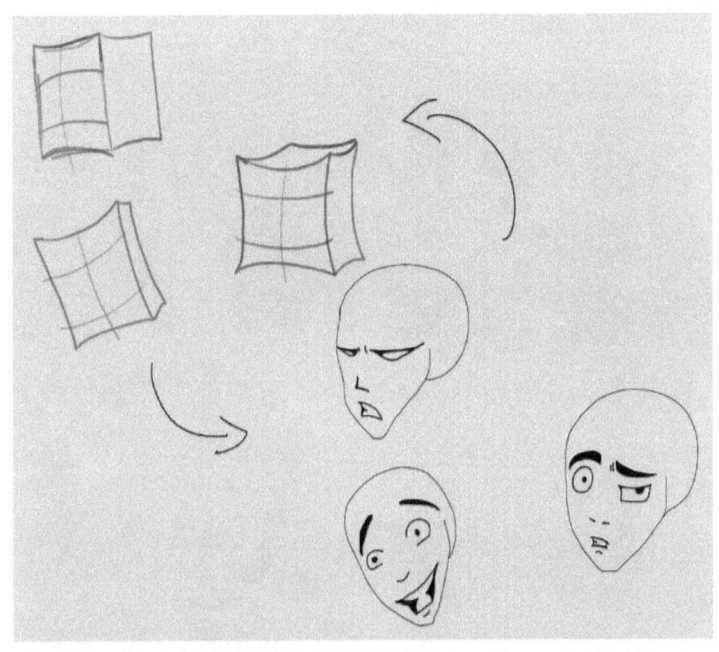

The next step to give more intensity to your characters, is to give it more dramatization. The easiest way to do it is to draw first to the character and then drawing you while you look in a mirror.

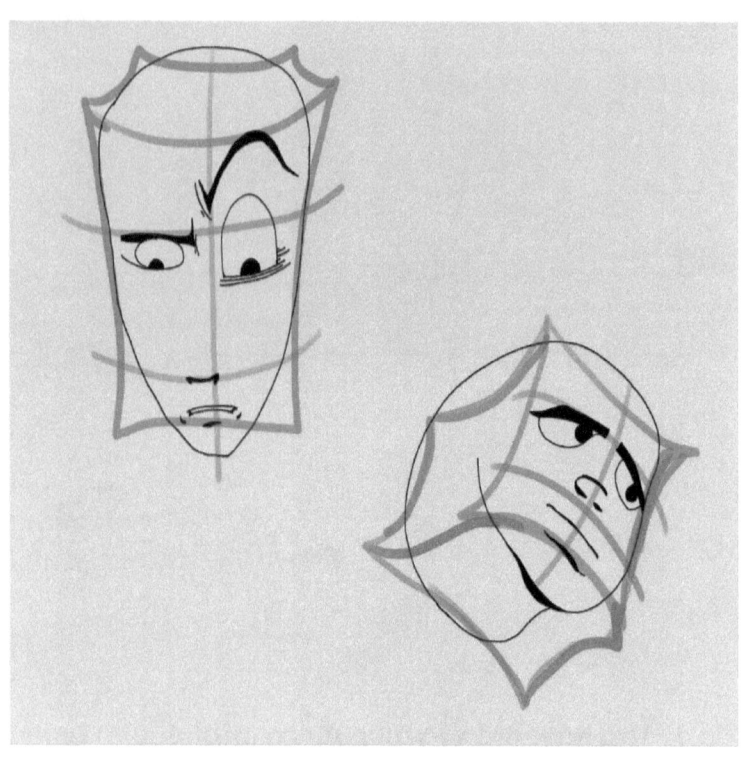

Make funny or exaggerated faces and draw them
in your character remember to exaggerate the movement
of the eyebrows and the mouth, that will help you when
run out of ideas.

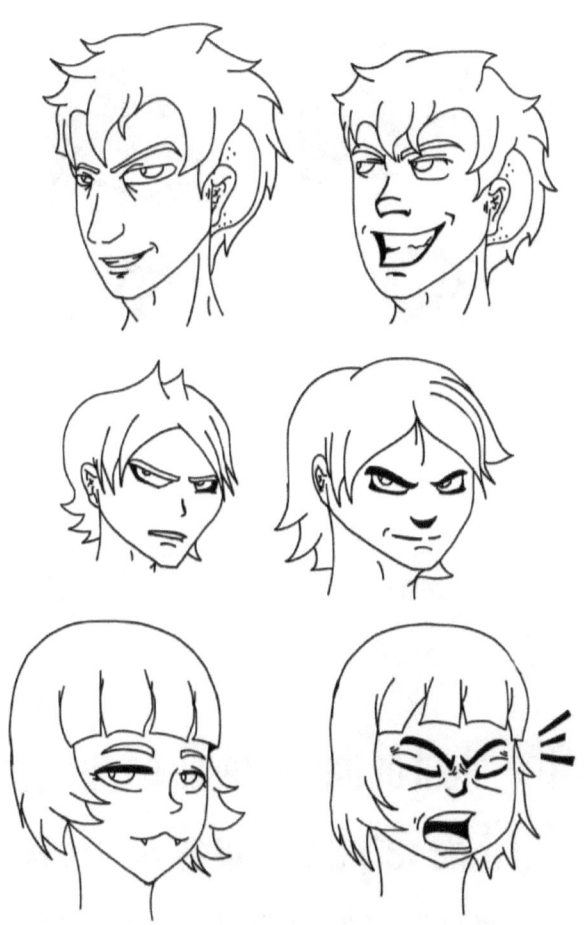

Using the eyebrow marking technique,
expressions can be further emphasized.

13

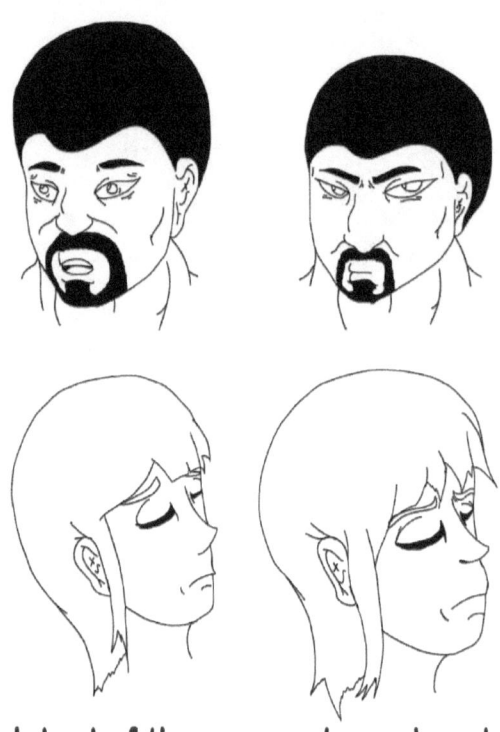

The intent of the expressions also change
if we vary the point of view of our
He drew; if a girl is sad, draw her
seen from above increases the sensation
of sadness.

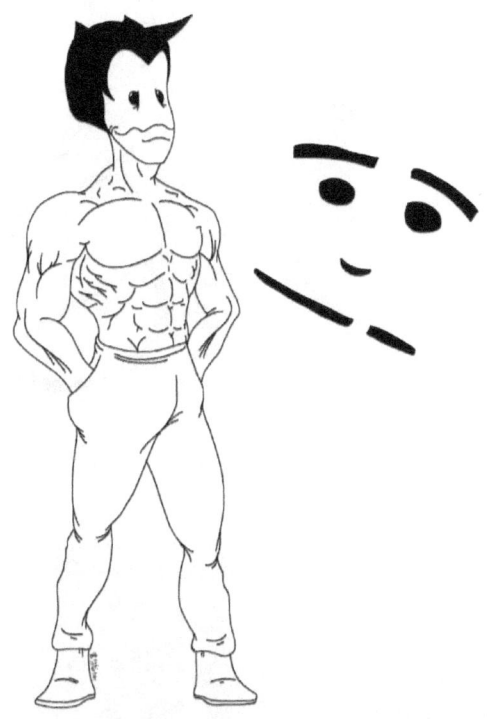

Some body positions also tell us
the mood of the character.
In this example we can define the character
as calm, carefree. Your line
Movement is slightly curved backwards.

15

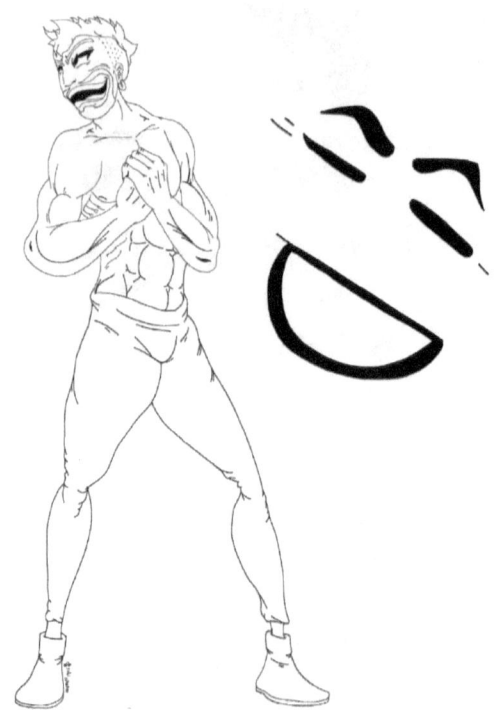

In this characterization of joy,
the line of movement is totally more
charged back, apart from movement
of the face, more specifically of the eyebrows,
eyes and mouth.

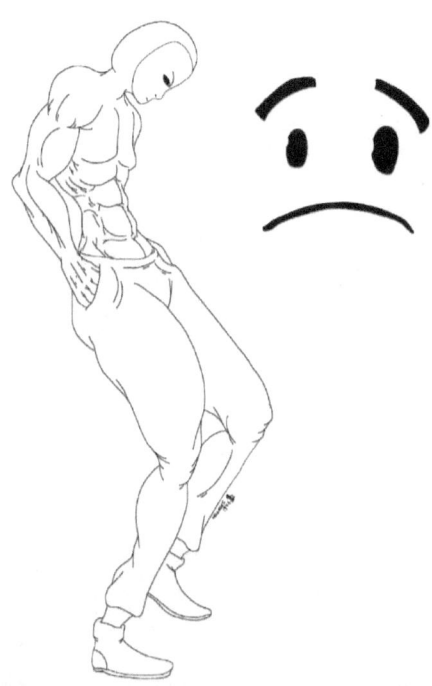

This position simulates sadness, the line of
movement is more curved but in this
dramatization the line moves forward.
The gaze is lowered as is the head. This
It must be a characteristic that must be
accentuate more both on the face and on the body.
17

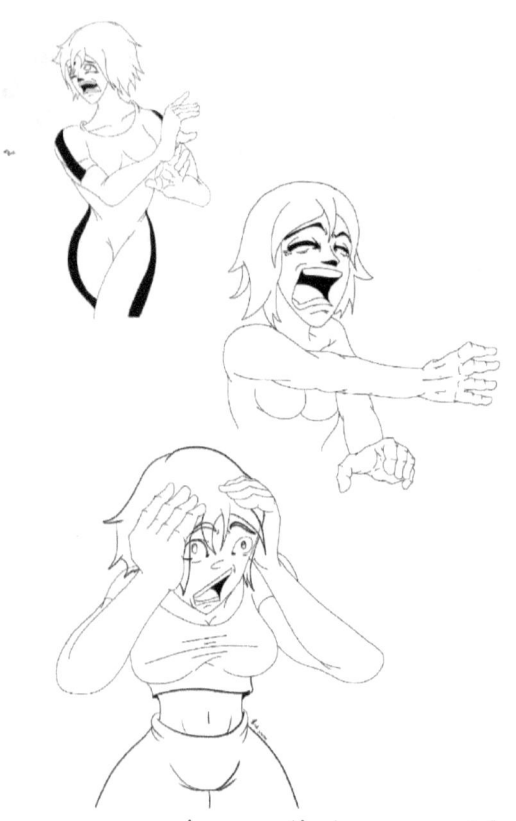

These are some images that represent fear,
the important detail that makes the receiver
understand the message is the face, where we should
accentuate eyebrows and mouth.

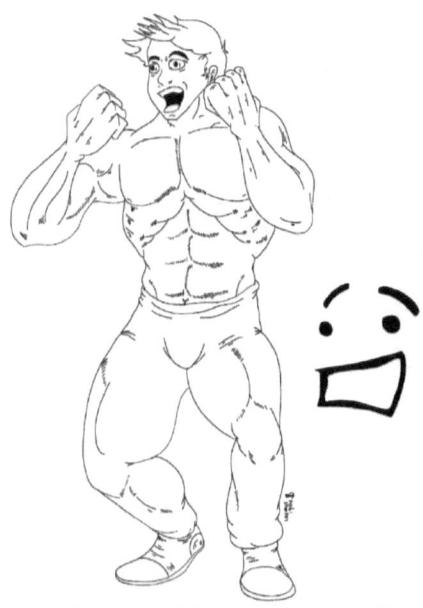

In this image I wanted to give you an intention
of fear of the character; just like the pose
sadly we can handle the line
forward motion.
This feeling is one that we should work on
and accentuate more, since sometimes we do not give
enough intention and the viewer doesn't get to
believe what we draw.

19

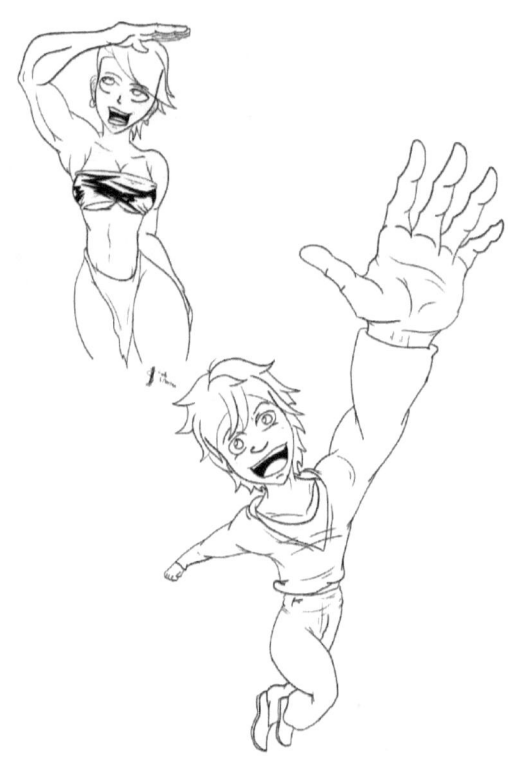

When we draw the characters with an expression
of happiness (which is made up of eyes, mouth and eyebrows),
eyebrows rise slightly, mouth opens more than
normal and the corners of the mouth move to
lateral parts of the face.

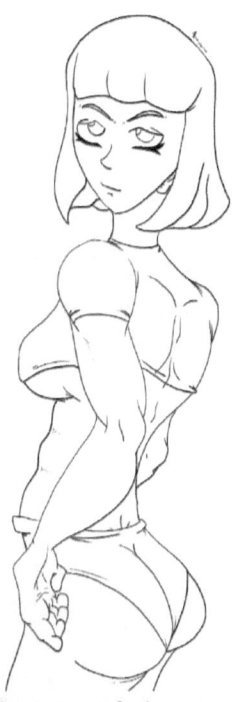

Also in the case of character design,
it is important to emphasize the most important details
but especially based on personality.
It is always important to remember that in the same way
in which we do not know the gender of a child, in the drawing
You must first put the behavior and then the gender.

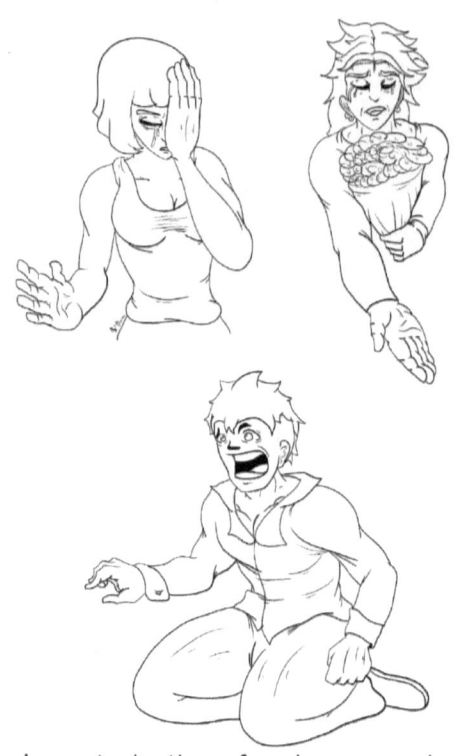

In the characterization of sadness, you have to work
plus the line of the eyebrows, since in the part of the frown
the wrinkles that are made are more noticeable, and the
eyebrows move from bottom to
above, ending in the middle of the forehead.

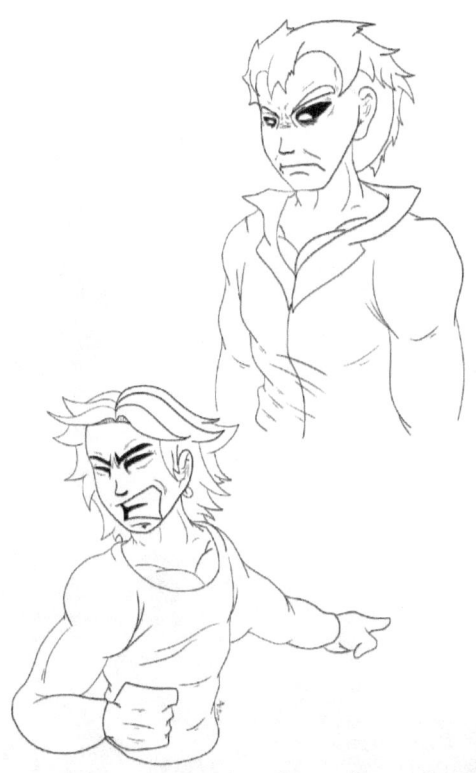

If your character needs a fury characterization
or angry, we should consider the eyes marking
the lower part with heavy shadows, then the eyebrows
they go down in the central part of the face, at the end
the mouth and teeth contract to improve expression.

To have a more spectacular attitude, you have to make a good image product in a good illustration, and give it a good character design. The line of movement must have good attitude, and you have to give plans to the drawing on paper.

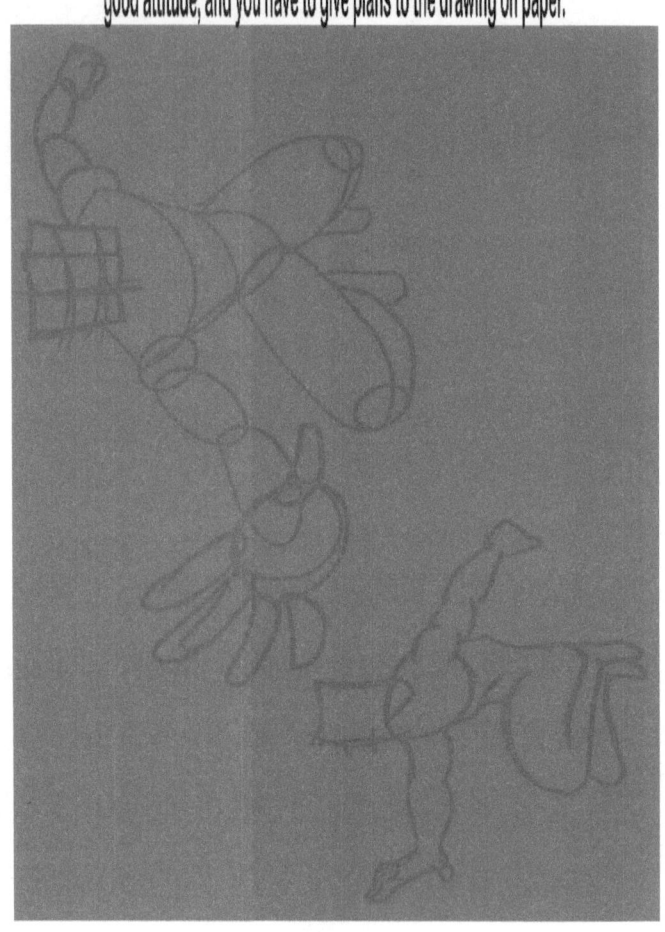

In the image you can see the hand in the foreground and the rest of the body goes into the background. This is called "foreshortening", which in short it means giving a drawing three dimensions on a flat surface.

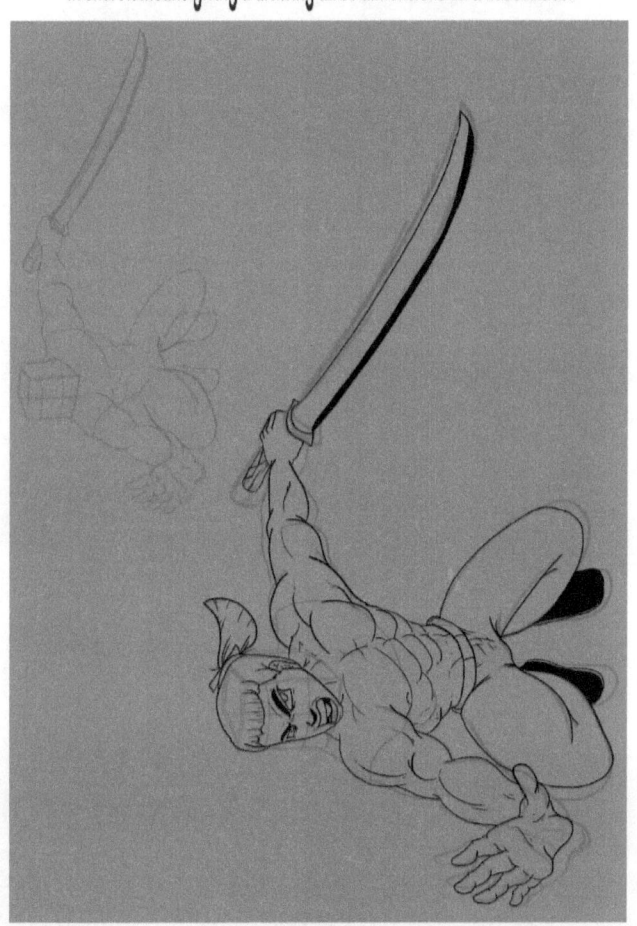

Foreshortening can only be given in drawing, painting and low relief, in these images
you can see the process of the stroke line. When drawing a foreshortening, the closest part to us is
large compared to the furthest point, where things become small.

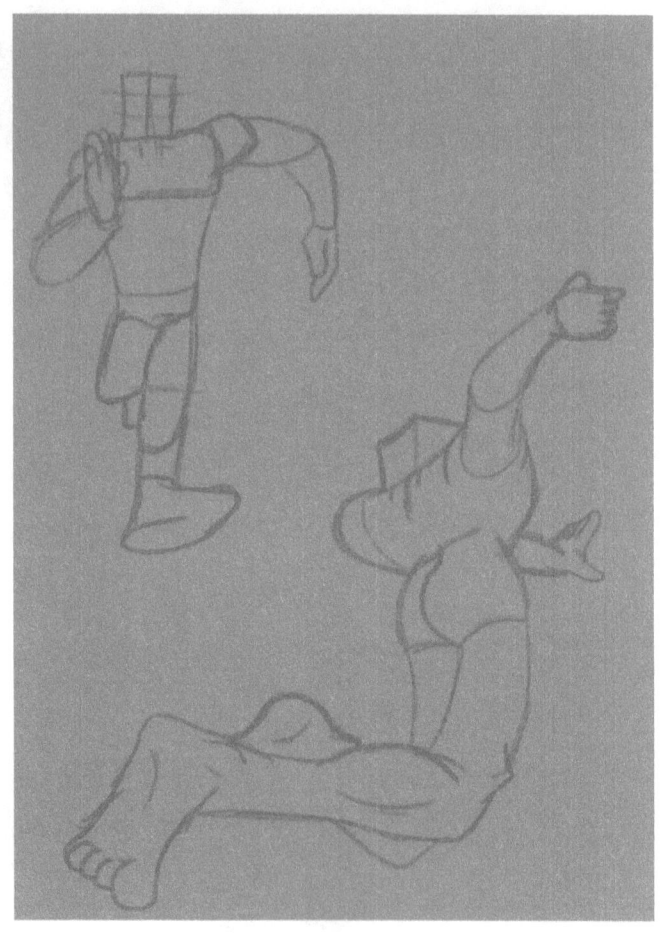

26

In this image we see how two bodies interact, the furthest body is small with reference to the closest body, the body that is in the foreground is bigger, but the hand is even bigger, since it is the closest point to us. Also the thickness of the line helps us to mark the foreshortening, the closest has a thicker line.

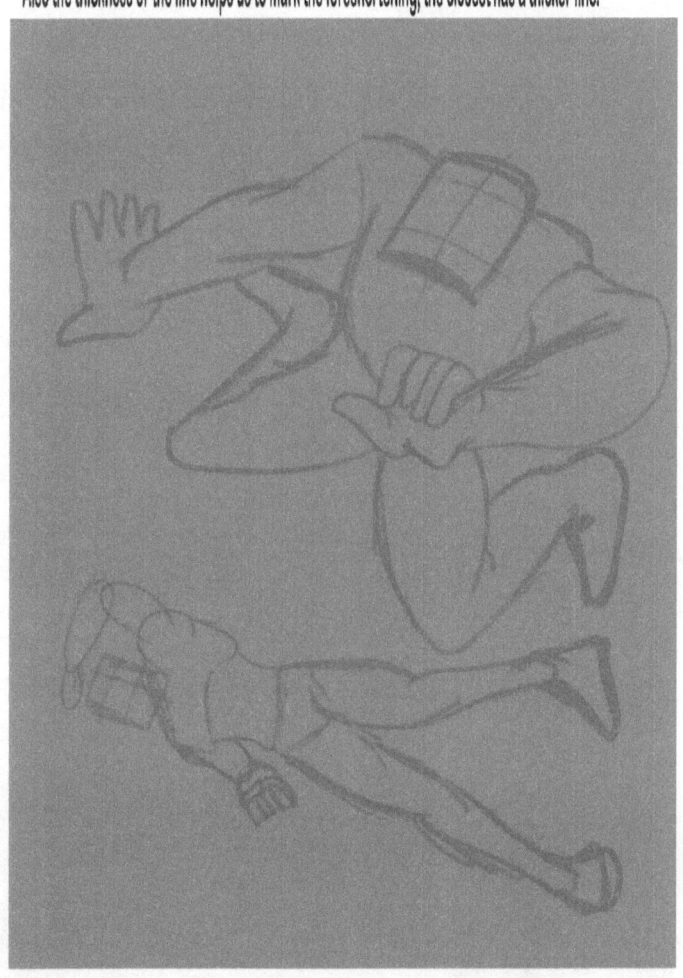

When the drawing is more sketched, the stroke looks erratic, contrary to the drawing with the defined line.
At the end of some exercises, we can understand this step in the drawing, according to the attitude of the face
it is the attitude of the body and vice versa. In this broken down drawing, we can clearly understand it by the feet,
Since the foot that performs the action is larger than the support foot, another important point is the line of the line.

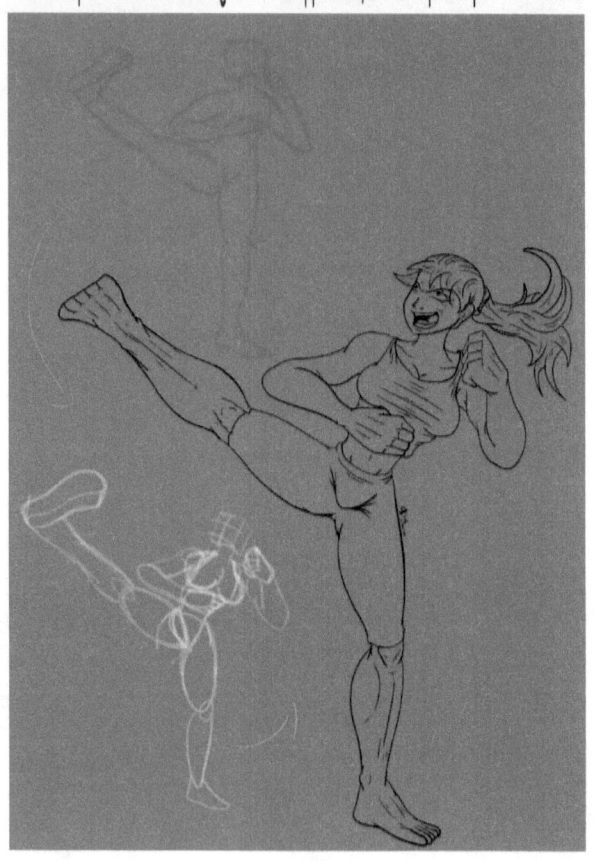

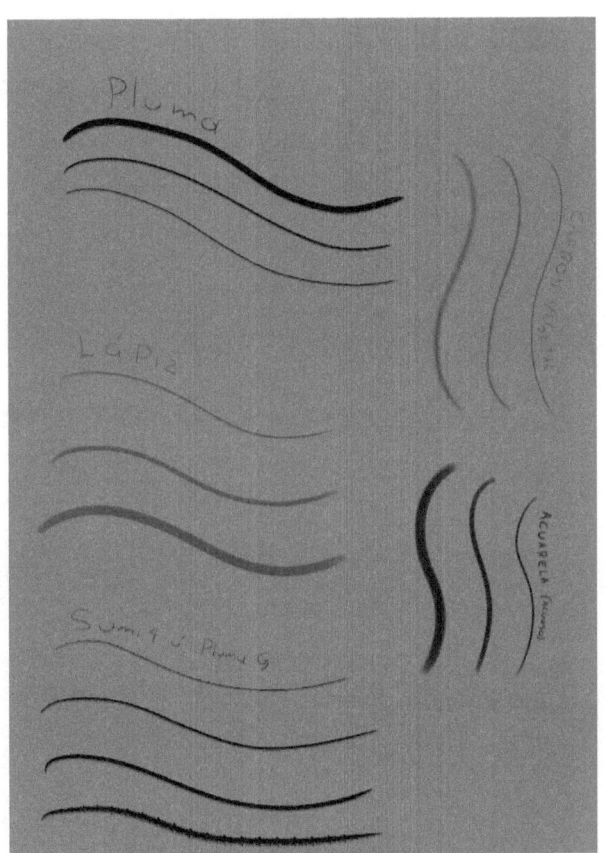

The trick to drawing with personality is knowing how to make a perfect line.

The first thing is to do these exercises that are seen on the page, using different materials in this case we see the line

pen, pencil, charcoal, watercolor (aqueous), sumi 4 or G pen.

Mostly the exercises are with the base to create a clean path and without so much tremors, to give

the expected result to work.

When drawing, we must move from the shoulder to the pencil, to make fluid movements. This is an exercise where we see the imaginary point where it would start to trace where it ends. Some exercises like zigzag or that starts with waves also help us.

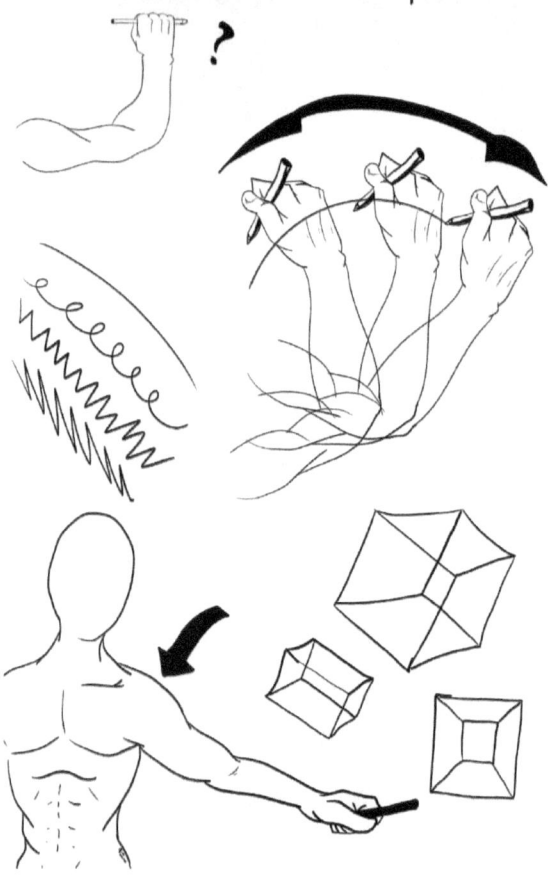

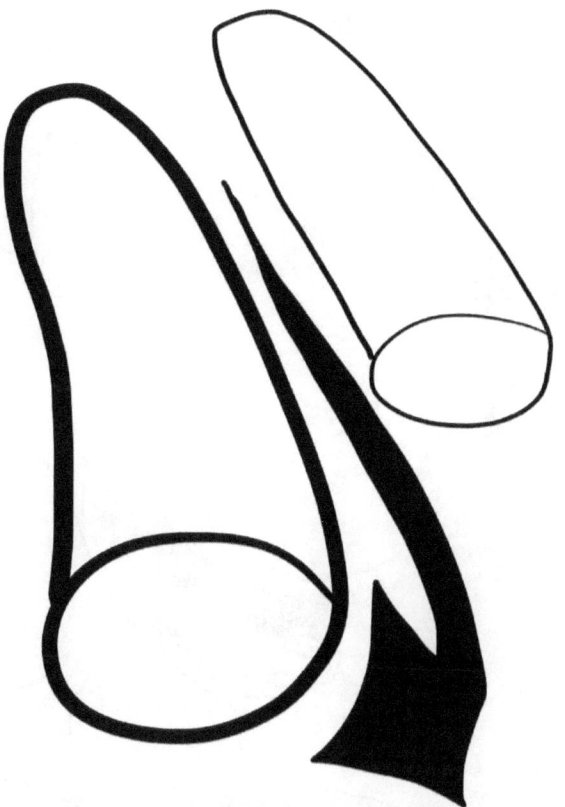

This is a clear example of what we can
do with the line and a foreshortening.
It is clearly seen that the part closest to
us, the line, looks thicker compared
from the farthest point where the line
he stayed with his family.

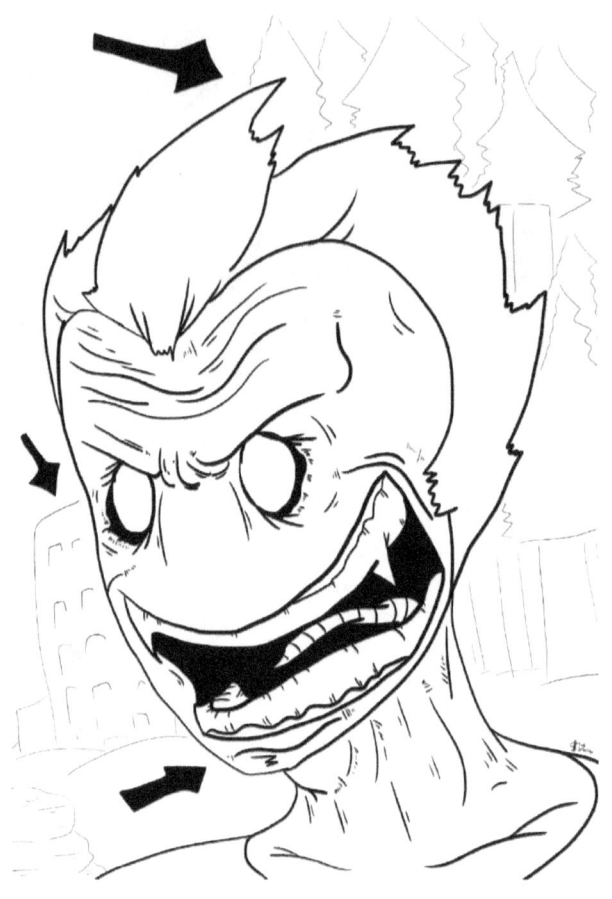

Another example of the line is the clipping, used to differentiate the main character in contrast with backgrounds or other designs.

The clipping line is regularly
used in the "Toon" style and consists
in making the outline of our
I draw somewhat thicker than the rest.

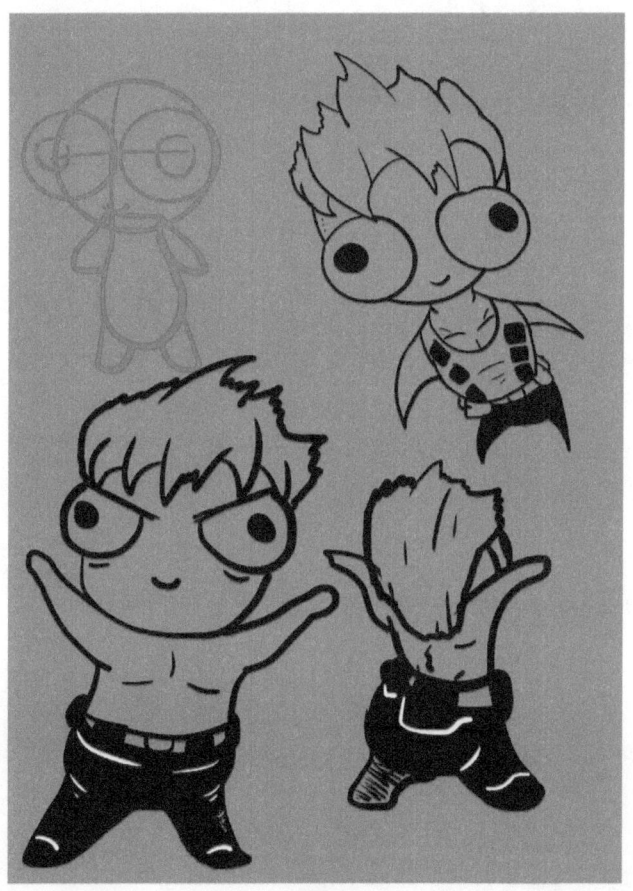

33

The thick line is also a consequence of the effect light and shadow.

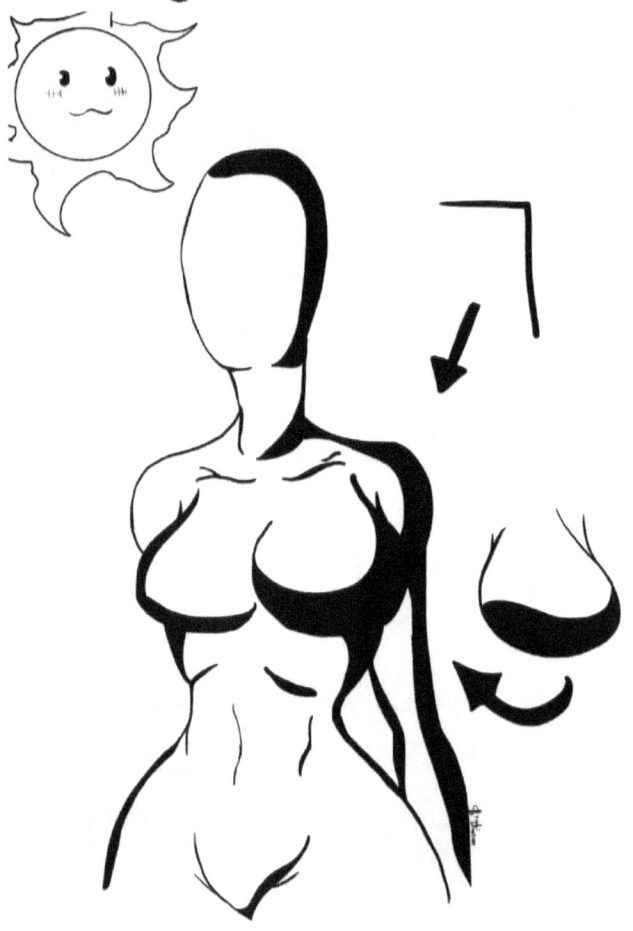

34

This example is the consequence of the stroke shape, the line becomes more thick as it loads towards the right as the curves are more loaded to the left side.

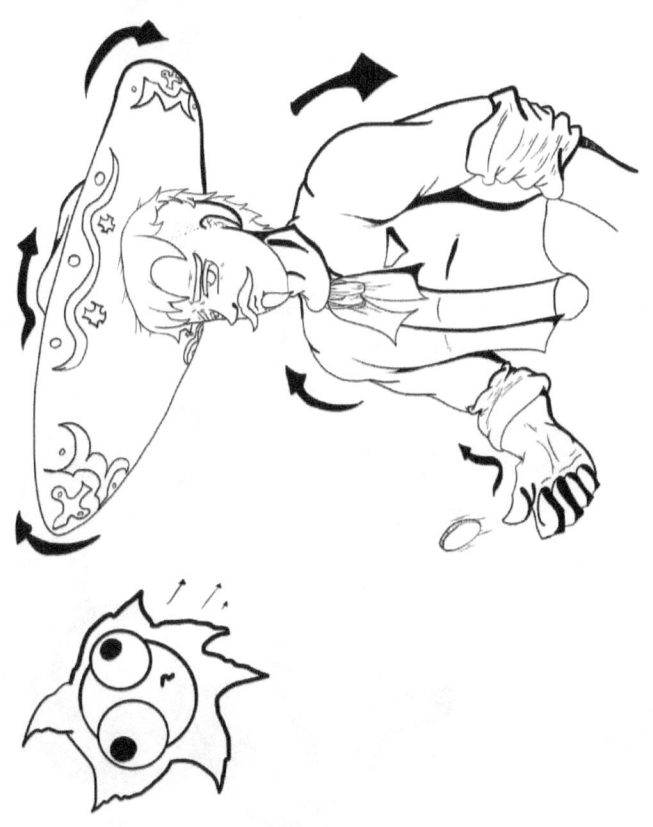

The following example is a
consequence of light and shadows.
By working in high contrast with the
ways we can give volume
no need to color or put
gray tones.

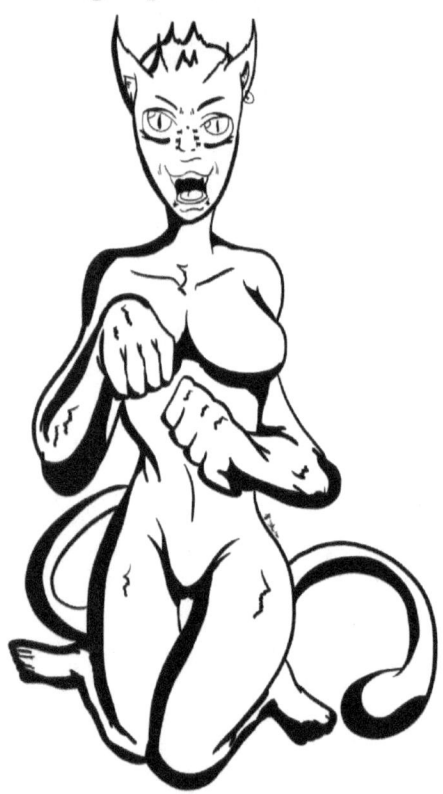

Another example using just thick and thin on the line.

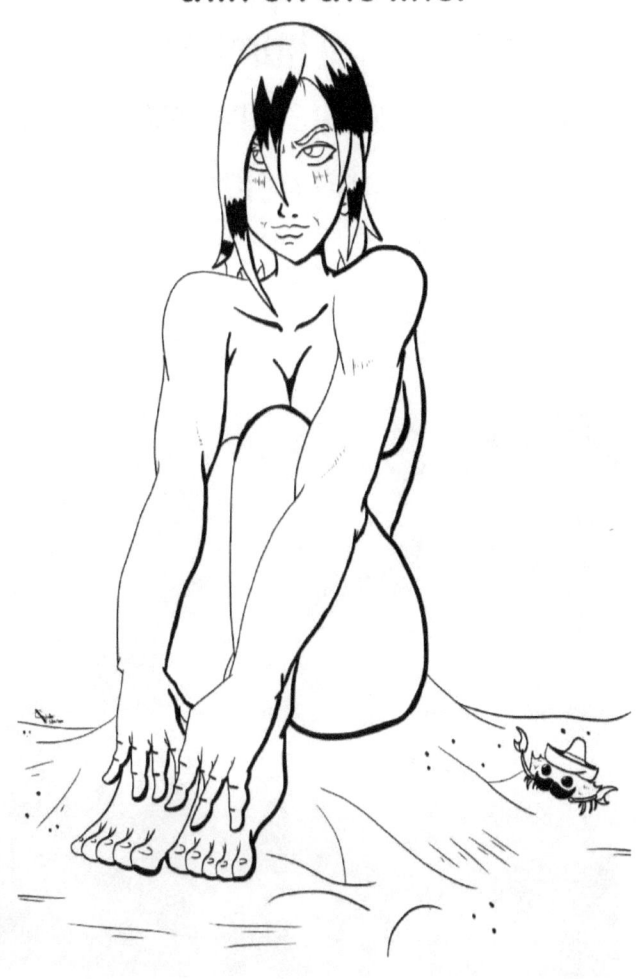

The next step to give you more presence to your character is to vary from a typical human figure to a with better structure, musculature and height.

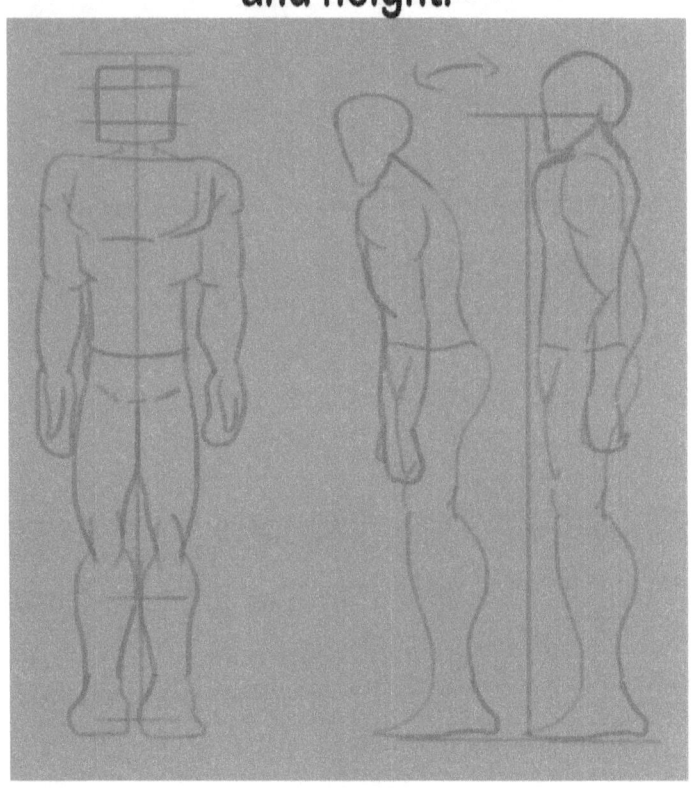

The line of movement or the line central is the one that carries the body weight of the character.

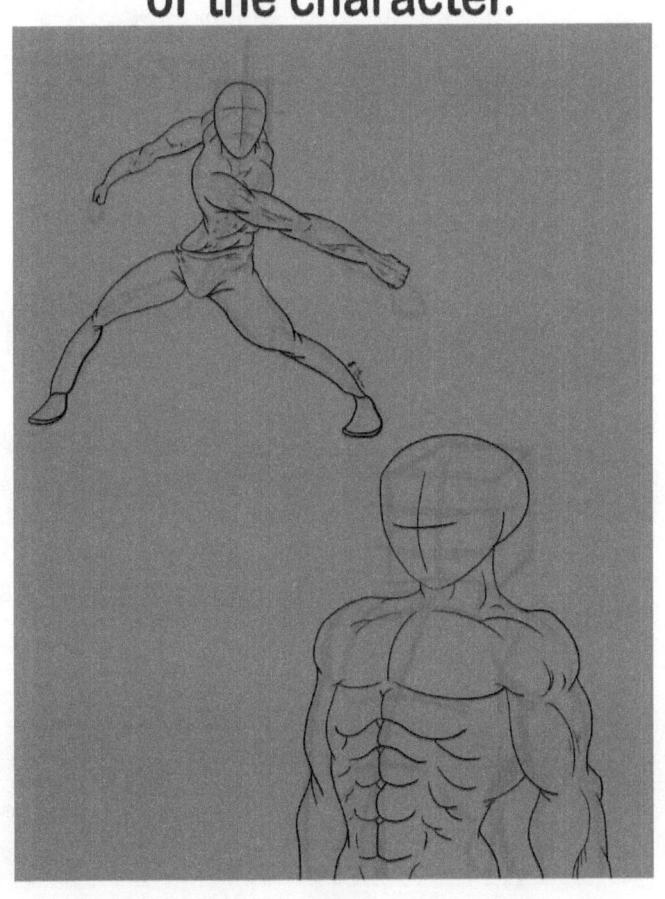

It is necessary to learn to manage the line of movements,
it is essential to be able to carry out
more striking or moving drawings
more exaggerated. As always, practice
is the important thing to progress in
the evolution of your work.

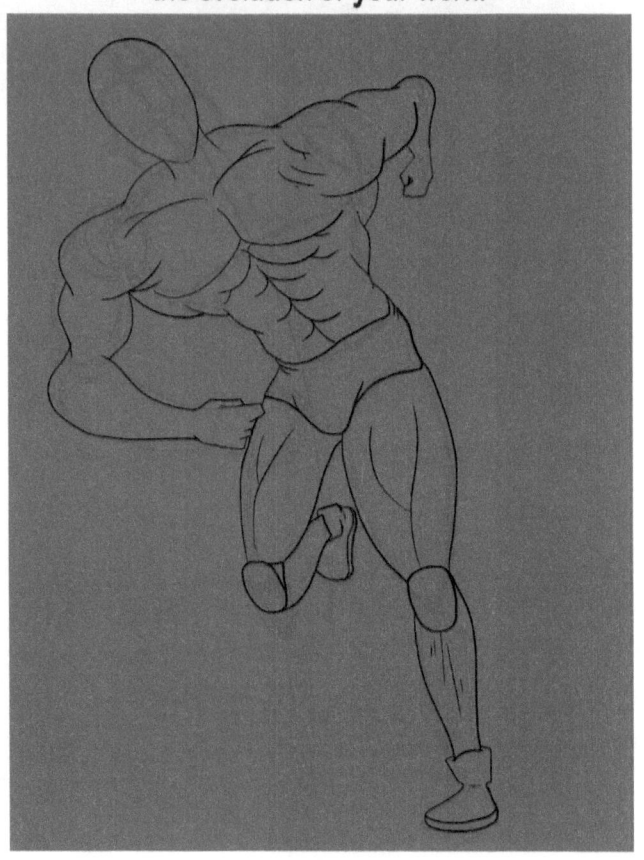

40

Now we will work on the design ...

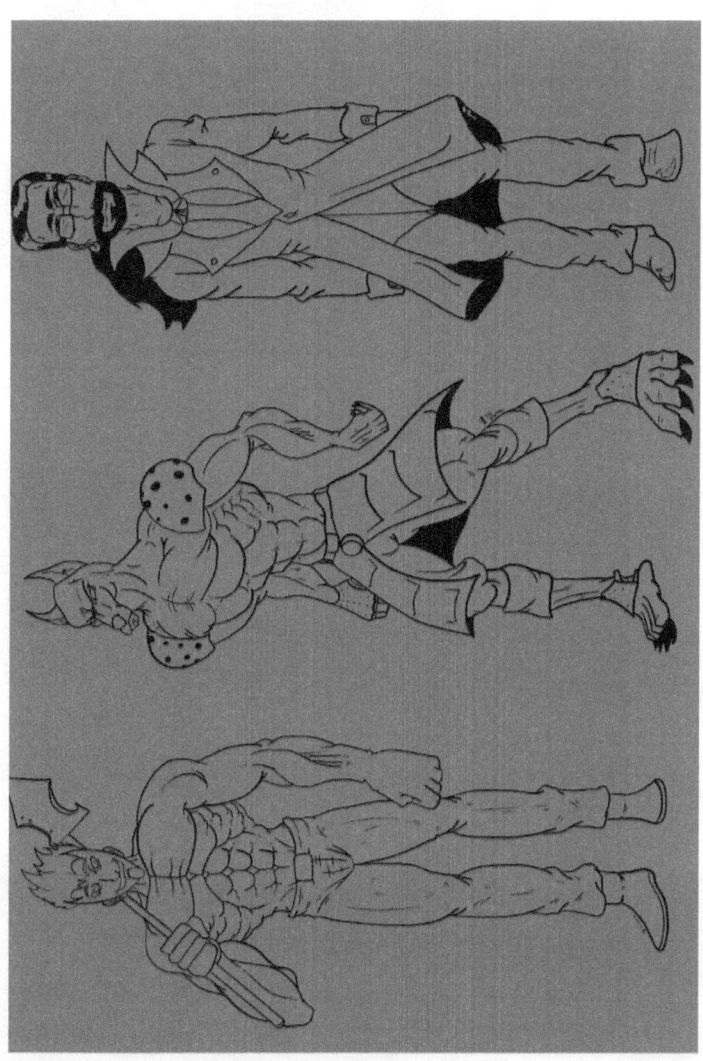

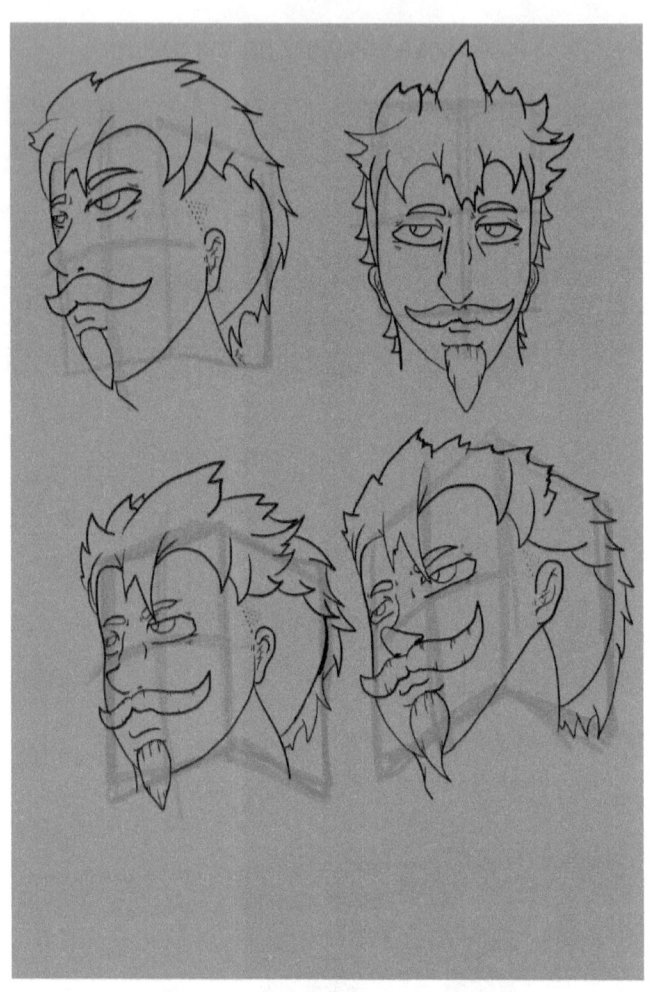

Practicing the previous exercises
we can carry out the design of the characters.
The first thing is to look for a characterization of the face.

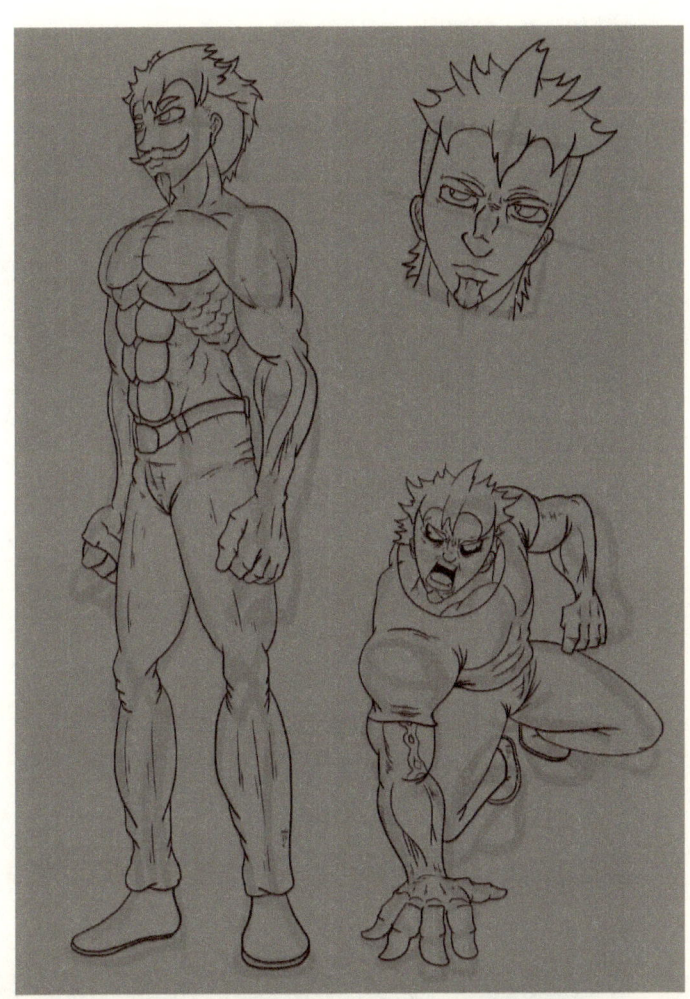

These are examples of a line stroke and
movement in which we carry out the
processes we've been seeing.

43

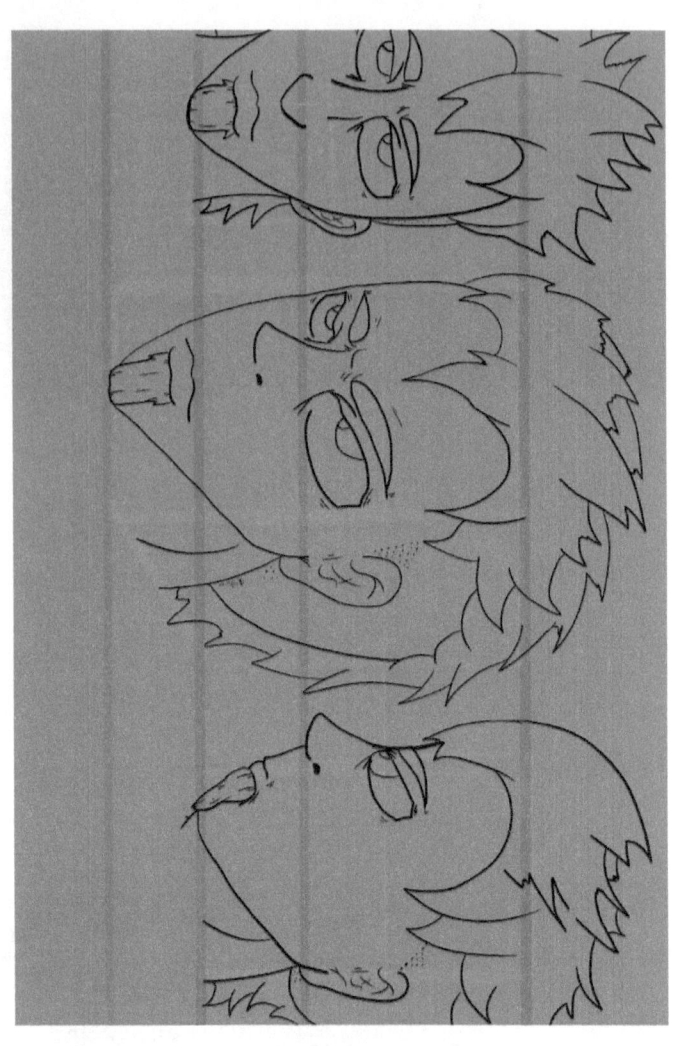

The next thing is to draw in three views, which are more recurring. These are front, profile and three-quarters.

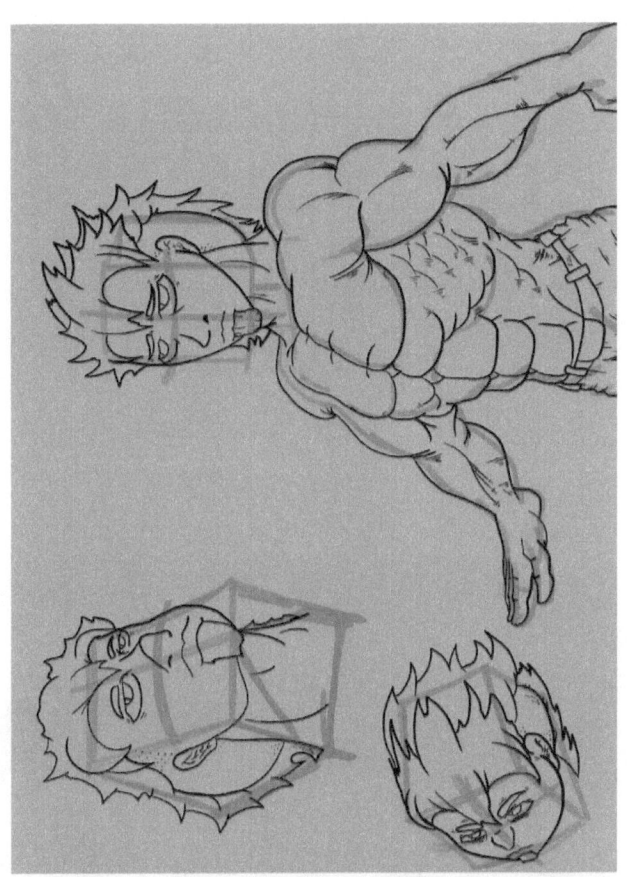

Next we will draw the face of the character
at various angles, since we must have a notion
of how the character looks at different angles.
Knowing how the face is, we will design the body
full. This is an action character,
so the character must be athletic.

45

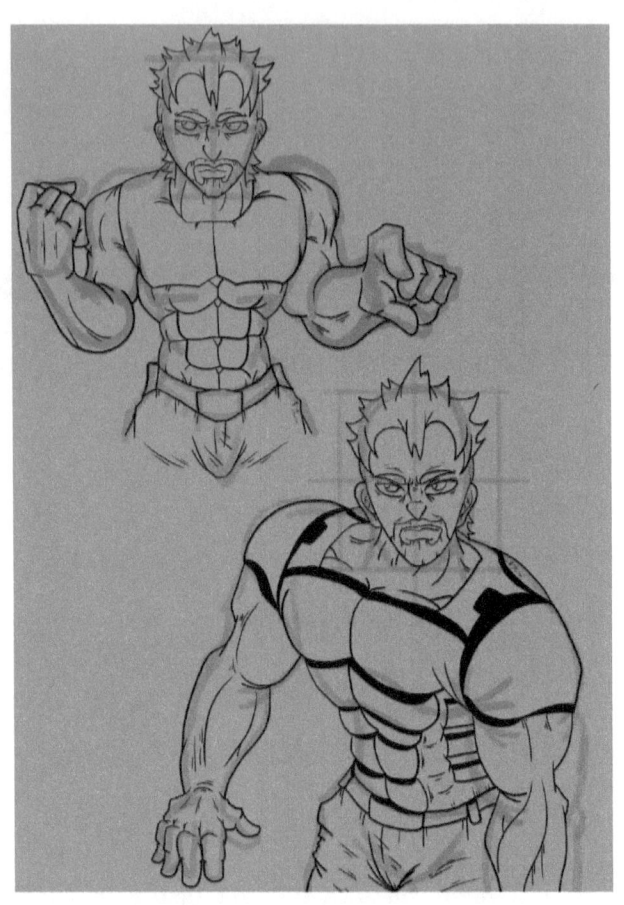

Let's make the character act.
The first images represent anger,
the two images show how the character
is unhappy, it shows through the mouth, because
looks tense.

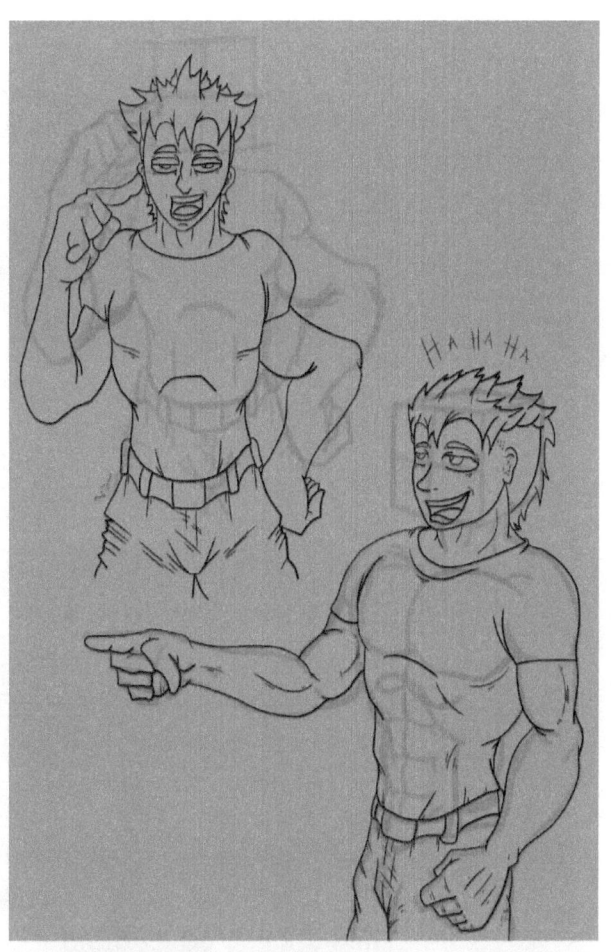

Now happiness. Although we can give
certain expression in the eyes, all these
expressions are emphasized with the mouth,
Well, we can't see the eyes or the eyebrows.

47

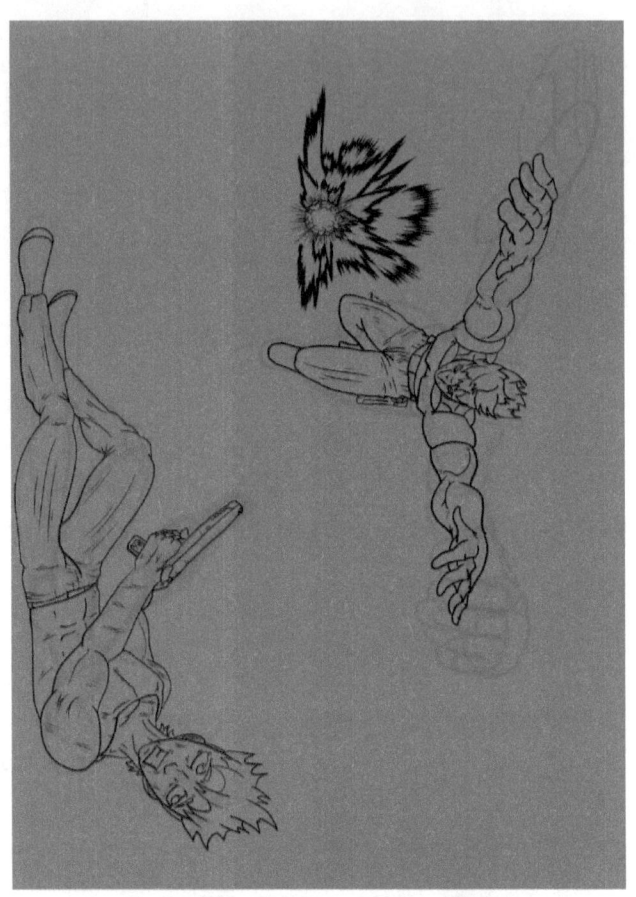

Fear, like the two sensations
above, it is represented the same in the
face features but this process
fear can be accentuated by
body movements.

48

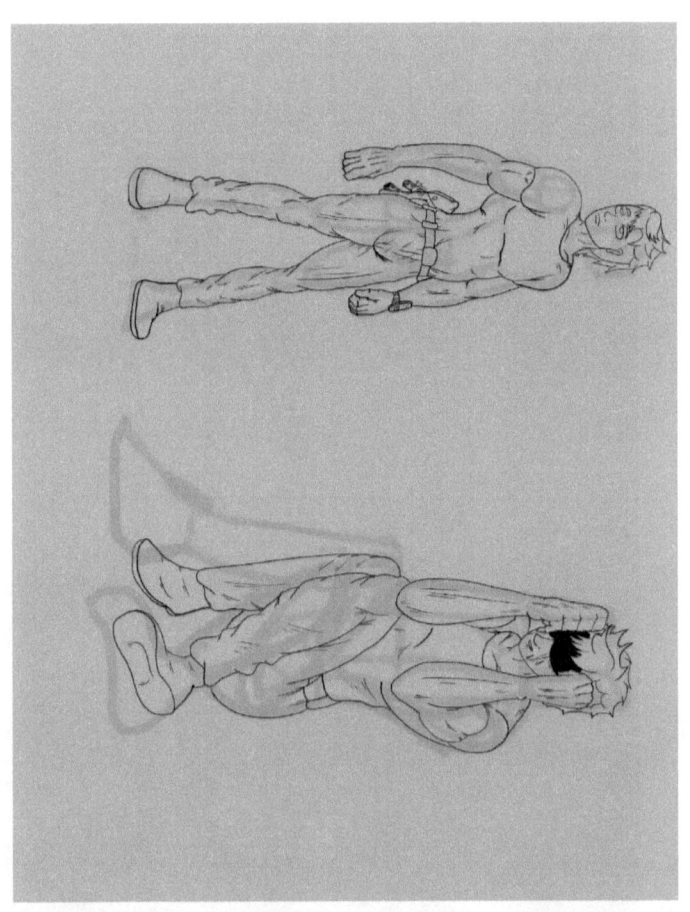

Something important that I forgot to mention is that
when we make a character be masculine
or feminine, you have to take the essence of gender:
pride, sexy, dramatic, courage,
vanity, awkwardness, etc.

49

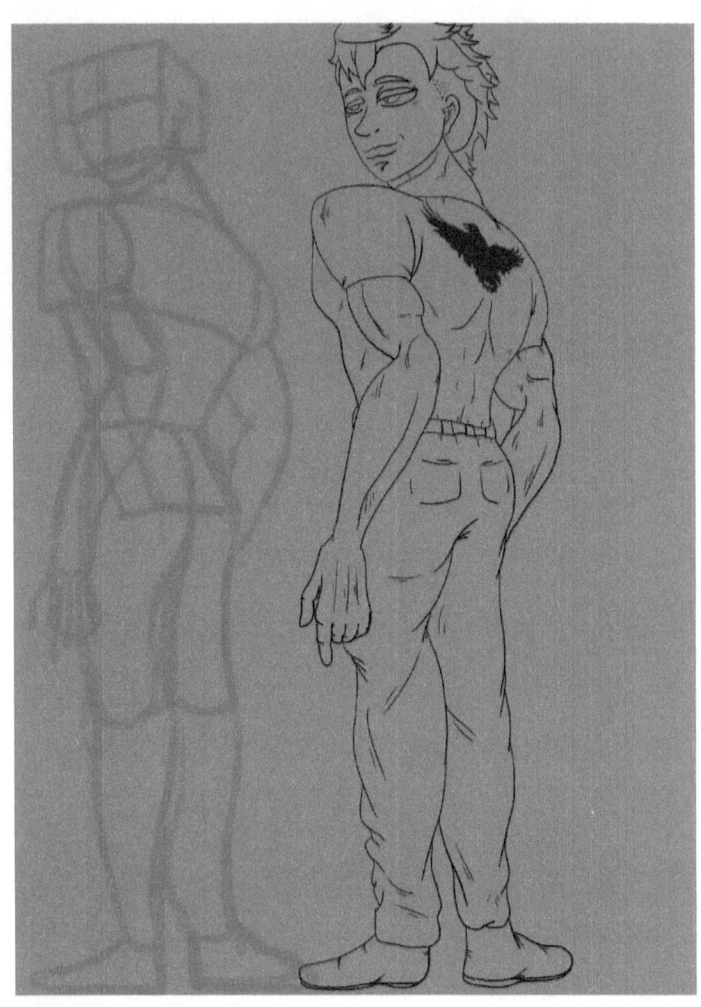

However, the characteristic must be maintained
main of each character. If he is a warrior,
it will all be summed up to his primary work.

50

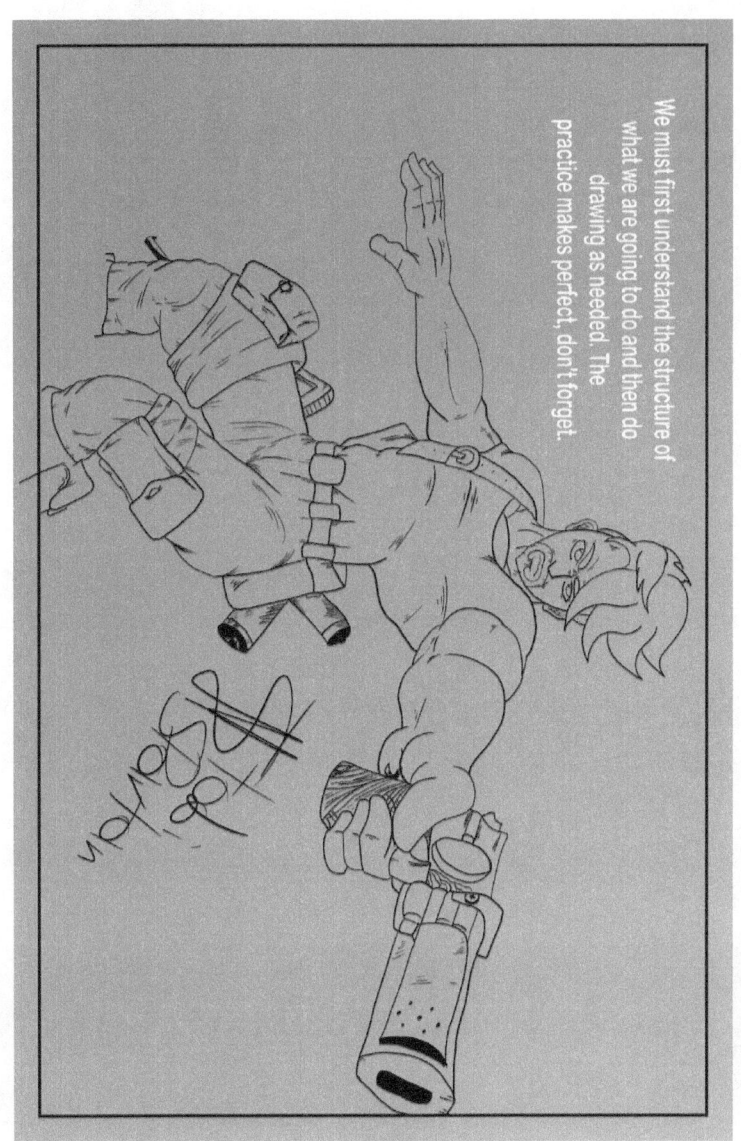

We must first understand the structure of what we are going to do and then do drawing as needed. The practice makes perfect, don't forget.

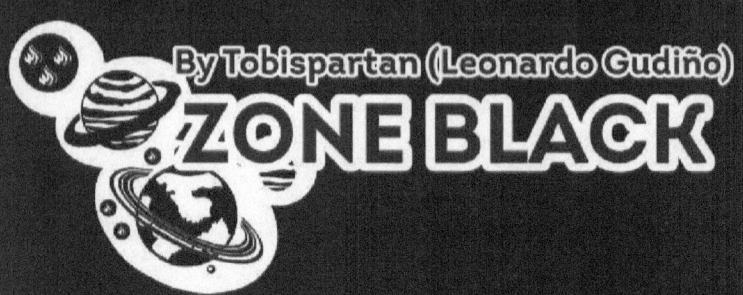

By Tobispartan (Leonardo Gudiño)

ZONE BLACK

More from the Author:

♥ Tao of Drawing

★ Basic Manual on graffiti

★ Zone Black Root

★ Unfair Fantasy Unfair Kat

♥ The day of Area 51

★ The Art of War Unveiled

www.ingramcontent.com/pod-product-compliance
Lightning Source LLC
Chambersburg PA
CBHW030532220526
45463CB00007B/2807